© Peter Cramer | MICEboard PUBLISHING
ISBN: 9798879130546

Peter is a distinguished b2b tourism and MICE sector expert specializing in elevating the digital presence of MICE suppliers across Germany, Austria, and Switzerland. Understanding the unique challenges of the industry, Peter addresses the overlooked need for direct sales engagement and bridges gaps in social selling and online content marketing.

Offering bespoke services to MICE suppliers, Peter's expertise benefits tourism boards, convention bureaus, event venues, hotels, and other service providers aiming to connect with German-speaking event planners.

Confronting industry challenges such as limited content creation time, insufficient publication knowledge, language barriers, and ineffective outreach, Peter provides comprehensive solutions:

- Expert B2B tourism and MICE consulting.
- Tailored content creation for the DACH market across various digital platforms.
- Exclusive MICE sales events targeting German-speaking buyers.
- Access to MICEboard community for impactful marketing.
- Hybrid sales strategies combining online and event-based approaches.

With a proven track record of successful collaborations and a commitment to enhanced visibility and business growth through advanced multimedia advertising solutions, Peter Cramer is your go-to for expanding your business in German-speaking Europe.

Peter Cramer
Hamburg

Hamburg in February 2024

Thank you very much for your support, especially Sayuri, who is always on hand with help and advice and supports me wholeheartedly. This book is dedicated to her.

Special thanks to Jörn Raith for the inspiration and template for the title of this book.

Note cover photo / author photo:
The cover photo was created with the help of artificial intelligence (PeC / Canva / Magic Media). The photo of the author was edited with the help of AI.

PROLOG

Charting Unexplored Territories in the MICE Industry.

As the dawn breaks over a transformed global landscape, the Meetings, Incentives, Conferences, and Exhibitions/Events (MICE) industry stands on the precipice of a new era, teeming with unprecedented challenges and boundless opportunities. This book is a compass to navigate the uncharted waters of this dynamic sector, promising to illuminate paths less trodden and unlock secrets to mastering the art and science of modern event planning and sales.

Embark on a journey through these pages as we delve deep into the heart of the MICE industry, unearthing the fundamental shifts brought forth by global events such as the Covid-19 pandemic, and the relentless march of digital evolution. Witness the metamorphosis of traditional event formats into innovative, hybrid marvels that blend the physical with the digital, creating immersive experiences that transcend geographical boundaries and conventional limitations.

In a world where change is the only constant, this book offers a beacon of knowledge and insight, guiding event planners, sales professionals, and industry stakeholders through the complex maze of modern MICE sales. Explore the intricate tapestry woven by advanced strategies such as content marketing, storytelling, and social media, which, when masterfully applied, can revolutionize the way we conceive, plan, and execute events.

Prepare to be intrigued by the profound transformation of traditional sales tactics into a sophisticated 'Hybrid Sales' model, a paradigm shift that promises to redefine the industry's future. As you turn these pages, you will be invited to question the status quo, challenge the conventional, and embrace the innovative. You will discover how to harness the power of hybrid events, creating platforms that not only facilitate connections but also foster meaningful interactions and enduring relationships.

This book is not merely a collection of insights and best practices; it is a clarion call to all MICE industry professionals to rise to the occasion, to adapt, innovate, and lead in an ever-evolving landscape. It is an invitation to embark on an exciting voyage of discovery, to learn, to grow, and to succeed in crafting events that resonate, engage, and inspire.

As you stand at the threshold of this adventure, let your curiosity be your guide, and your passion for excellence be your driving force. The journey ahead is fraught with challenges, but it is also ripe with opportunities to leave an indelible mark in the annals of the MICE industry. Welcome to a journey of transformation, innovation, and success.

Welcome to the future of MICE hybrid events (sales).

TABLE OF CONTENTS

WHO IS THE BOOK FOR

This book is meticulously crafted for a diverse array of professionals within the dynamic sphere of the MICE industry. It is an essential resource for:

Event Planners and Coordinators: Whether you are orchestrating corporate conferences, elaborate exhibitions, or intimate incentives, this book offers a treasure trove of insights on how to elevate your events through hybrid formats, ensuring they are not only memorable but also foster meaningful connections and engagement.

MICE Sales Professionals: Sales experts within the industry will find invaluable strategies and innovative approaches in these pages, particularly regarding the shift to 'Hybrid Sales'. The book guides you in harnessing the power of content marketing, storytelling, and social media to not just reach but resonate with your audience.

Marketing Executives in Hospitality and Tourism: Professionals charged with marketing destinations, venues, or services for MICE activities will discover cutting-edge tactics to position their offerings advantageously in a market that is increasingly digital yet craves personal connections.

Corporate Decision-Makers: Business leaders who recognize the value of meetings and events as catalysts for company growth, employee engagement, and stakeholder relationships will find this book a strategic asset. It offers a fresh perspective on integrating hybrid events into your corporate communication and marketing strategies.

Academics and Students in Event Management: Educators and learners alike will appreciate the book's rich content, which provides a current view of industry trends, digital transformation, and the evolution of event sales and planning - crucial knowledge for the industry's future trailblazers.

Technology Innovators and Solutions Providers: For those who are at the forefront of providing or seeking new technological solutions for the MICE industry, this book sheds light on the actual needs and potential applications of technology in creating impactful, engaging, and seamless event experiences.

Industry Consultants and Thought Leaders: As a thought-provoking resource, the book offers fresh insights and perspectives that can inform consultancy practices, keynote speeches, and strategic guidance for clients in the MICE sector.

In essence, this book is for anyone with a stake in the future of the MICE industry, offering a comprehensive guide to navigating, innovating, and succeeding in an ever-evolving landscape where the blending of digital and physical experiences is not just an option, but a necessity for growth, engagement, and enduring success.

DEFINITION OF HYBRID EVENTS

Hybrid events signify a pivotal shift in the realm of Meetings, Incentives, Conferences & Exhibitions/Events (MICE), epitomizing an innovative amalgamation of physical and digital experiential worlds. These events are designed to transcend the boundaries between the real and virtual realms, crafting a seamlessly integrated overall experience.

Hybrid events are ingeniously structured to merge the benefits of physical in-person gatherings with the versatile capabilities of digital platforms. Unlike traditional in-person events, which necessitate attendees' presence at the venue, or entirely virtual events accessible solely online, hybrid events curate an integrated experience. They empower participants to engage actively in the event, irrespective of their geographical location or prevailing circumstances.

A quintessential feature of hybrid events is the duality of the participant experience. The events are meticulously tailored for both attendees present on-site and online participants. Through the deployment of cutting-edge technologies and imaginative conceptual design, it is ideally ensured that both cohorts relish an equitable, interactive, and enriching event experience.

STRATEGIC SIGNIFICANCE OF HYBRID EVENTS

The strategic importance of hybrid events in the MICE sector is multifaceted. On one hand, they broaden the scope of events by overcoming barriers such as travel expenses, time constraints, and physical distances. This expansion leads to an increased number of participants and a more diverse audience. On the other hand, hybrid events provide a platform for broader interaction and networking, breaking through the conventional limits of physical events.

Furthermore, hybrid events enable comprehensive data analysis and targeted engagement with participants. The digital component allows for the collection of valuable data concerning attendee behavior, preferences, and interactions. This data serves as a crucial resource for the continual enhancement of event concepts and the creation of personalized experiences.

Hybrid events represent a forward-thinking evolution in the MICE industry, offering a plethora of opportunities to supplement and expand traditional event formats. They signify an adaptation to the evolving needs and expectations of participants, reflecting the ongoing digitalization and connectivity of our world. For providers in the MICE sector, integrating hybrid events presents an opportunity to diversify their offerings, extend their reach, and create a comprehensive, inclusive, and interactive event experience. In an era where flexibility, accessibility, and innovation are key, hybrid events provide a platform that meets these demands, propelling the MICE industry into the future.

BUT IS THAT REALLY THE CASE?

In the event industry, hybrid events are defined in three main variants, each offering unique approaches and possibilities:

- **Dual-Participation Model**: The dual-participation model presents an advanced and flexible solution for organizing and conducting events, crucial in today's increasingly digitalized world. This model acknowledges the needs and preferences of a broad spectrum of participants by providing a hybrid structure that integrates both physical and virtual participation options.

In the dual-participation model, attendees have the option to be present in person at the event venue or participate virtually via digital platforms. This duality allows for the best of both worlds: the immediacy and personal connection of physical presence, along with the convenience, accessibility, and reach of virtual participation.

The physical component of the model emphasizes the importance of personal contact and direct interaction. This approach promotes networking, idea exchange, and the creation of synergies in a shared physical environment. Participants can experience not only lectures and presentations but also engage in face-to-face interactions during breaks and social events, often leading to more profound discussions and long-term partnerships.

Concurrently, the virtual component provides a flexible and inclusive alternative. Participants unable to be physically present due to geographical, temporal, or financial constraints have the opportunity to access the content in real-time or at a later stage. The use of digital technologies such as live streaming, interactive Q&A sessions, and virtual networking spaces enhances the participation and engagement of virtual attendees. This significantly extends the event's reach, making it accessible to a global audience.

A crucial aspect of the dual-participation model is ensuring a high-quality experience for both groups of participants. This requires meticulous planning and the implementation of specific technical solutions to ensure that both the physical and virtual components are seamlessly integrated, providing an interactive, engaging, and valuable experience for all involved.

In summary, the dual-participation model represents an innovative response to the dynamic requirements of the modern event industry. By combining the advantages of physical and virtual participation, it offers a versatile and inclusive platform that meets the needs of a diversified audience, expands the boundaries of participation, and creates a rich and interactive event experience.

- **Hub-and-Spoke Model**: The Hub-and-Spoke model represents a revolutionary approach in organizing and conducting events, with the potential to fundamentally transform the dynamics of interaction and communication in a global context. Originating from the transport and logistics sector, where it serves to optimize routes and enhance distribution efficiency, this model now finds innovative application in the event industry.

At the heart of the Hub-and-Spoke model are concurrent local events, serving as "Spokes," digitally connected to a central "Hub." This Hub acts as a pivotal point, not only linking the individual Spokes but also serving as a central platform for content, interaction, and communication. This structure creates a decentralized event that occurs simultaneously in different locations, yet is unified through digital technologies within a cohesive framework.

A key advantage of the Hub-and-Spoke model is its ability to elevate local events to a global level. Participants can engage in a local event tailored to their specific regional needs and interests while being part of a larger, globally connected community. This structure not only fosters local engagement and involvement but also broadens participants' horizons by providing access to a wider range of content and discussions.

Furthermore, the Hub-and-Spoke model offers a platform for enhanced interactivity. Digital tools such as live streaming, chat functions, and interactive workshops allow participants to be actively involved in the proceedings, regardless of their location. This interactivity is further amplified by the ability to exchange content and experiences in real-time between the Spokes and the Hub, creating a dynamic and responsive event environment.

In conclusion, the Hub-and-Spoke model not only represents an innovative solution for conducting events in an increasingly connected world but also responds to the growing demand for flexible, interactive, and inclusive event formats. In an era where digital technologies are redefining how we communicate, learn, and interact, this model offers a forward-looking platform that leverages local strengths while simultaneously building global bridges.

- **Pre- and Post-Event Virtual Extensions**: The concept of pre- and post-event virtual extensions represents an innovative expansion in the realm of event organization, aimed at maximizing participant engagement and involvement before and after a physical event, such as a congress. Although less prevalent in the context of hybrid events, this strategy offers unique advantages and opportunities to strengthen interaction and community spirit among participants, thereby enhancing the value of the main event.

Pre-event virtual extensions primarily serve to build a community and prepare participants for the upcoming physical event. Organizing online meetings, webinars, or interactive discussion forums allows organizers to create a platform where participants can get to know each other, form networks, and familiarize themselves with the content and objectives of the main event. This phase is crucial for arousing interest and expectations and laying a solid foundation for community building. Moreover, the pre-event phase enables effective communication of essential information, such as agenda updates, logistical details, or introductions to key topics, ensuring that participants are better prepared and more motivated for the actual event.

Post-event virtual extensions, on the other hand, focus on the follow-up of the physical event. They provide a platform to deepen the insights gained during the main event, continue discussions, and further promote networking. This phase can offer additional content such as recordings of speeches, summaries of workshops, or exclusive interviews with speakers, allowing participants to catch up on or delve deeper into content they may have missed. Post-event virtual extensions also provide space for feedback sessions, offering organizers valuable insights for improving future events.

A critical advantage of this modular event structure is the reduction in the no-show rate. The continuous engagement and motivation of participants before and after the event create a stronger bond and commitment to the event.

Participants feel part of a community, increasing the likelihood that they will indeed attend the physical event and actively participate, transforming from mere attendees to active contributors.

In summary, the model of pre- and post-event virtual extensions represents a comprehensive strategy that can significantly enhance the value of a physical event. By creating a continuous and engaged participant experience that extends beyond the actual event, these complementary virtual phases foster the development of a strong community, intensify content exchange, and maximize the overall impact and sustainability of the event.

The integration of pre- and post-event virtual extensions into the format of a physical event, such as a congress, represents a strategic innovation that aligns with the needs of modern, connected, and information-driven societies. Particularly for closed participant groups, where targeted communication and interaction are crucial, these hybrid event structures offer significant advantages. The relevance of this model is justified by various key elements and their influence on event design and perception.

One of the main arguments for implementing pre- and post-event virtual extensions is the efficient dissemination of content, thereby reaching a conscious participant group. Traditional communication channels can often be limited in today's world dominated by digital media. In contrast, hybrid events provide a platform that not only improves the reach and accessibility of content but also enables targeted addressing and preparation of participants.

For instance, the MICEboard.com community, a leading online portal and network for the German-speaking MICE market in the DACH region, strategically utilizes pre- and post-event virtual extensions to ensure continuous and focused communication. Through targeted storytelling and interactive online communication, a solid foundation for participant decision-making is established. This is particularly relevant for event planners and international providers wishing to participate as exhibitors. By clearly communicating relevant information, expectations, and opportunities in advance, potential participants can make an informed decision about their attendance, enhancing the quality and relevance of the participant group at the actual event.

Moreover, the model of pre- and post-event virtual extensions enables a deeper and more sustainable engagement experience. Before the actual event, participants can develop an understanding of the thematic focuses through virtual meetings, webinars, or interactive forums, ask questions, and network with other participants and exhibitors in advance. After the event, virtual follow-up events provide a platform to continue discussions, present additional content, and deepen networking.

Using this extended event model significantly contributes to reducing the no-show rate and maximizing the investment in the event. The continuous and targeted engagement of participants fosters stronger bonds and a greater commitment to the event and its objectives. This not only leads to higher attendance and engagement rates but also creates a stronger and more enduring community that extends beyond the single event.

The model of pre- and post-event virtual extensions to a physical event represents a relevant and meaningful expansion of the traditional event format. By creating an integrative and continuous participant experience that extends beyond the actual event, not only are participant engagement and commitment maximized, but a stronger, more informed, and engaged community is also established, securing the long-term success of the event.

THE EMERGENCE OF HYBRID EVENTS

Within the ever-evolving landscape of the event industry, hybrid events occupy a pivotal role. They are not merely a trend emerging from technological advancements in recent years and the repercussions of the COVID-19 pandemic but are the result of a dynamic evolution driven by various factors. A central element in this development is technological progress. This chapter delves into the role of technology in shaping and implementing hybrid events and discusses its significance for the MICE (Meetings, Incentives, Conferences, and Exhibitions/Events) industry.

Technological advancements have revolutionized the way events are conceptualized, organized, and experienced. The integration of digital platforms, sophisticated audio-visual equipment, and interactive tools has made it possible to create immersive and engaging hybrid event experiences. These events seamlessly blend the physical and virtual worlds, catering to both on-site participants and remote audiences.

The role of technology in hybrid events is multifaceted. Firstly, it facilitates broader access and participation. With the aid of live streaming, virtual reality (VR), and augmented reality (AR), participants can engage with the event from any location, overcoming geographical and logistical barriers. This global reach not only expands the audience base but also enhances the event's inclusivity and diversity.

Secondly, technology serves as a powerful tool for engagement and interaction. Interactive features such as live polls, Q&A sessions, and networking platforms allow virtual participants to be active contributors rather than passive viewers. This interactivity ensures that the virtual experience is as enriching and dynamic as the physical one, fostering a sense of community and connection among all participants.

Moreover, technology enables sophisticated data collection and analytics. Event organizers can track participant behavior, preferences, and engagement levels through various digital touch points. This wealth of data provides valuable insights for tailoring content, optimizing future events, and demonstrating return on investment (ROI) to stakeholders.

However, the successful implementation of hybrid events requires more than just technology; it demands a strategic approach and meticulous planning. Event professionals must ensure that the technology serves the event's objectives and enhances the participant experience. This involves selecting the right technological tools, designing engaging content, and providing support to participants unfamiliar with digital platforms.

In conclusion, the emergence of hybrid events marks a significant milestone in the evolution of the event industry. Powered by technological innovation, these events offer a versatile and inclusive platform that transcends traditional boundaries. As the industry continues to navigate through changing times, hybrid events stand as a testament to the resilience, adaptability, and forward-thinking approach of the MICE sector.

TECHNOLOGICAL ADVANCEMENT AS A CATALYST FOR HYBRID EVENTS

The advancement of technology, particularly in the realms of digital communication and live-streaming services, has laid a solid foundation for the emergence and proliferation of hybrid events. High-definition video transmission and interactive tools have opened the doors to a new era of events that seamlessly blend physical and digital elements. High-resolution video broadcasting ensures that online participants enjoy an experience as immersive as those present on-site.

The quality of the transmission plays a crucial role in effectively and convincingly presenting the content. On the other hand, interactive tools and apps allow two-way communication between participants and organizers. Features such as live polls, Q&A sessions, or networking platforms actively involve online participants, offering a participatory and interactive event experience.

The integration of digital and physical experiences is another core component of successful hybrid events. The challenge lies in not just allowing both worlds to coexist but in linking them to create a cohesive overall experience. This requires thoughtful planning and the application of innovative technological solutions.

Technological advancement has not only expanded the possibilities for conducting hybrid events but also changed the expectations and requirements of participants and clients. Today, participants expect a high-quality, interactive, and seamlessly integrated event experience, whether they are physically present or connected online. For providers in the MICE industry, this means they must continuously engage with the latest technological developments and integrate them into their event concepts to remain competitive.

Technological progress plays a central role in the development and implementation of hybrid events. It not only enables the creation of a comprehensive and integrated event experience but also demands constant evolution and adaptation from the players in the MICE industry. In a world where technology is rapidly advancing, it is crucial to stay abreast of the times and creatively and effectively utilize the opportunities presented by technological progress to design unique event experiences.

The changing landscape in the MICE industry is shaped not only by technological advancement but also significantly by the changing expectations and requirements of participants.

In today's globally connected and fast-paced world, participants seek more flexible and individualized participation options. Hybrid events address this development by offering the choice between physical and digital participation. This chapter discusses how the changing participant expectations influence the design of hybrid events and what challenges and opportunities arise for the players in the event industry.

EVOLVING PARTICIPANT EXPECTATIONS AS A CATALYST FOR HYBRID EVENTS

Today's participants demand a high degree of flexibility and personalization in their event participation. The option to choose between physical or digital attendance not only extends the event's reach but also appeals to a broader audience. This accommodates the diverse needs and preferences of participants, whether they be related to spatial or temporal constraints, travel budgets, or personal preferences.

Hybrid events allow participants to decide how they wish to experience the event. While some prefer the personal interaction and direct experience on-site, others value the convenience and flexibility of online participation. This choice enhances the event's appeal and increases participant satisfaction.

The evolving expectations of participants present new challenges for providers in the MICE industry. Designing a hybrid event requires not only the technical and organizational capability to facilitate both forms of participation but also a deep understanding of the individual needs and desires of participants. A successful event is characterized by a coherent experience that meets the needs of both physically and digitally present participants.

At the same time, these changing expectations also offer opportunities for the MICE industry. Hybrid events enable reaching a larger and more diverse audience, thereby holding the potential to increase participant numbers and the visibility of the event. Furthermore, they open up new possibilities for data collection and analysis to better understand participant preferences and behaviors, allowing future events to be even more targeted and personalized.

These changing participant expectations are a key driver in the development and proliferation of hybrid events. They challenge the MICE industry to rethink and adapt their event formats but also offer the chance to tap into new audiences and enrich the participant experience. In an era where flexibility, individualization, and participant-centricity are crucial factors, hybrid events provide a platform that meets these demands and steers the MICE industry in a future-oriented direction.

The Imperative for Sustainable Action and Environmental Conservation as a Central Factor in Event Design and Execution. The necessity for sustainable action and environmental conservation has established itself as a pivotal factor in the design and execution of events. In the MICE industry, this growing consciousness is reflected in the increasing popularity of hybrid events. These events offer not only an innovative amalgamation of physical and digital participation but also proactively address the sustainability endeavors of the industry. This chapter illuminates the role of hybrid events in the sustainability efforts of the MICE industry and discusses the implications for organizers and participants.

SUSTAINABILITY ENDEAVORS AS A CATALYST FOR HYBRID EVENTS

Sustainability in the MICE industry manifests in the endeavor to design events that are as environmentally friendly and resource-efficient as possible. Hybrid events contribute significantly to this by notably reducing the need for physical travel. Especially international events, traditionally associated with a high volume of travel, benefit from this aspect. The option for online participation allows participants from around the world to engage without leaving a substantial ecological footprint through air travel or long car journeys.

The reduction in travel requirements leads not only to a decrease in CO2 emissions but also to a reduction in the overall resource consumption of the event. Less physical presence also means a very much lower demand for accommodation, catering, and physical infrastructures. These factors contribute to significantly diminishing the ecological footprint of an event and enhancing its sustainability profile.

For organizers, integrating hybrid events means adjusting their planning and organizational processes. They are challenged to incorporate both technological and ecological aspects into their event concepts. This requires not only technical expertise but also an awareness of eco-friendly practices and sustainable event design.

For participants, hybrid events offer the opportunity to actively contribute to a more sustainable event culture. Opting for online participation instead of physical travel is a conscious step towards reducing one's personal ecological footprint. At the same time, hybrid events allow participants to effortlessly engage in a variety of events and connect globally without significant inconveniences.

Hybrid events play a crucial role in the sustainability endeavors of the MICE industry. They provide an effective way to reduce the ecological footprint of events, thereby contributing to the creation of an environmentally friendly and resource-conserving event culture. For both organizers and participants, hybrid events offer the chance to actively participate in shaping a sustainable future. In an era where sustainability and environmental protection are key societal concerns, hybrid events represent an innovative and responsible option that meets the needs of the modern world and steers the MICE industry in a more sustainable direction.

Global Connectivity and the Potential of Digital Technologies as Fundamental Catalysts in the Event Industry. Global connectivity and the potential of digital technologies have fundamentally transformed the event industry. Hybrid events, in this context, represent a progressive development that transcends the geographical boundaries of traditional events and enables worldwide participation. This chapter sheds light on the significance of the global reach of hybrid events for the MICE industry and outlines the resulting opportunities and challenges for organizers and participants.

GLOBAL REACH AS AN OPPORTUNITY

The incorporation of digital elements in hybrid events allows organizers to extend their audience beyond local and national borders. The digital component of these events enables participants from around the world to engage and take part, regardless of their geographical location. This global reach opens up new dimensions of international collaboration and networking, creating a platform for the exchange of knowledge, cultures, and ideas on a global scale.

For businesses and organizations, hybrid events provide an opportunity to reach an international audience and enhance their brand presence on a global level. By participating in internationally oriented hybrid events, they can increase their visibility in new markets and forge valuable connections with international partners and potential clients. The global orientation of hybrid events also brings specific challenges. Organizers are tasked with creating content and programs that are relevant and appealing to an international audience. In addition, they must overcome technical and organizational challenges, such as bridging time differences and providing multilingual content.

Despite these challenges, hybrid events offer tremendous potential for the MICE industry. They enable organizers to design their events in a way that meets the needs of a globally connected and diverse society. Hybrid events can help overcome cultural barriers, foster international partnerships, and promote a deeper understanding and greater acceptance among different cultures and communities.

The global reach of hybrid events represents a significant development in the MICE industry. It opens up new opportunities for international collaboration and networking for organizers and participants, contributing to the expansion of the boundaries of traditional events. In an increasingly connected world, hybrid events offer a platform that overcomes geographical restrictions and brings people together from all corners of the globe. For the MICE industry, this means the chance to take a leading role in shaping a globally integrated and collaborative event culture.

Recent global events, particularly the Covid-19 pandemic, have underscored the importance of crisis resilience in the MICE industry. In this respect, hybrid events have proven to be an adaptive and robust format of events, offering a valuable alternative during times of uncertainty and restrictions. This chapter explores the role of hybrid events in maintaining the continuity of business and educational activities under challenging circumstances and discusses the significance of crisis resilience for the event industry.

CRISIS RESILIENCE AS A CORE COMPONENT OF HYBRID EVENTS

Hybrid events, with their dual structure combining physical and digital participation, offer a flexible and resilient solution for conducting events. They allow for a response to unpredictable circumstances such as travel restrictions, health crises, or other disruptive events without the need to completely cancel the event. This ensures that business and educational activities can continue even under challenging conditions.

The adaptability of hybrid events enables organizers to respond swiftly to changing conditions and ensure the safety and well-being of participants. At the same time, they can maintain or even expand the reach and number of participants in their events by offering a participation option for a broad international audience.

The ability to successfully conduct events even in times of crisis is of strategic importance for the MICE industry. Hybrid events not only provide a solution for overcoming immediate challenges but also represent an investment in the long-term resilience and sustainability of the industry.

The crisis resilience of hybrid events helps to strengthen the confidence of participants, clients, and stakeholders. It signals that the industry is capable of responding flexibly and responsibly to changes and creating valuable event experiences even under difficult conditions.

Crisis resilience is a key feature of hybrid events and plays a crucial role in maintaining the continuity of business and educational activities. Hybrid events offer a flexible and robust solution to respond to unforeseen events and ensure the execution of events even in challenging times. For the MICE industry, this means the opportunity to position itself as agile, adaptable, and crisis-resistant and to take a leading role in creating a resilient and future-proof event culture.

The emergence of hybrid events thus also marks a significant evolution in the MICE industry. It represents an adaptation to the changing world where flexibility, accessibility, and resilience are paramount. Hybrid events embody the industry's commitment to innovation and its ability to evolve with the times, ensuring that the sector remains vital and relevant in a rapidly changing global landscape.

CHALLENGES IN CONDUCTING HYBRID EVENTS

While hybrid events offer a multitude of advantages, they also present event organizers and technical teams with a spectrum of challenges. The successful execution of a hybrid event demands meticulous planning, resources, and the navigation of specific obstacles.

Characterized by the fusion of physical and digital event components, hybrid events necessitate not only high-quality technology but also a stable and reliable internet connection. The aim is to provide both in-person attendees and online participants with a seamless and interactive experience. The challenge lies in managing the technical complexity inherent to this type of event.

Ensuring a high-quality and uninterrupted transmission is paramount, as any technical glitch or connectivity issue can significantly detract from the attendee experience. This requires a robust infrastructure, adept technical support, and contingency plans to address potential issues promptly. Additionally, orchestrating the seamless integration of live and virtual components involves intricate synchronization and real-time coordination, demanding a high level of technical expertise and meticulous attention to detail.

Moreover, delivering content that is engaging and accessible to both physical and virtual audiences is another critical challenge. This requires thoughtful content curation, dynamic presentation styles, and the use of interactive tools that transcend the physical-digital divide. Presenters and speakers need to be adept at engaging both audiences simultaneously, often necessitating training and rehearsal to refine their delivery for this unique format.

Furthermore, ensuring participant interaction and networking, integral elements of the event experience, poses a challenge in the hybrid format. Facilitating meaningful connections between in-person and online attendees involves innovative networking platforms and interactive sessions designed to foster engagement and collaboration across the physical-digital boundary.

Hybrid events also necessitate a nuanced understanding of audience dynamics. Catering to diverse participant preferences, managing varying time zones, and providing multilingual support are essential for creating an inclusive and accessible event environment.

In summary, while hybrid events embody a forward-thinking approach in the MICE industry, they bring forth a set of complex challenges. Tackling these involves a blend of technological prowess, strategic planning, and an empathetic understanding of participant needs. By successfully addressing these challenges, event organizers can harness the full potential of hybrid events, offering enriched, inclusive, and resilient event experiences that resonate with a global audience.

TECHNICAL COMPLEXITY AND RELIABILITY IN HYBRID EVENTS

Technical disruptions such as poor audio or video quality, internet connection interruptions, or the failure of interactive tools can significantly impair the participant experience and diminish the impact of the event. The quality of transmission and digital interaction is crucial for the success of a hybrid event, as they significantly influence participant satisfaction and engagement.

Strategies for Managing Technical Challenges

To tackle technical challenges and ensure a smooth experience for all participants, thorough planning, testing, and technical support are essential. Here are some key strategies:

1. Thorough Planning and Preparation: Detailed technical planning is the cornerstone of a successful hybrid event. This includes selecting the appropriate platforms and tools, ensuring a stable internet connection, and planning backup solutions for potential technical disruptions.

2. Technical Tests and Rehearsals: Comprehensive tests of the technical equipment and digital platforms should be conducted before the event. Rehearsals help to identify and rectify potential weak points in a timely manner.

3. Provision of Technical Support: A competent technical team available throughout the event is crucial for responding swiftly and effectively to technical challenges. This includes providing support for online participants to immediately address any technical difficulties they may encounter.

The technical complexity and the need for reliability present central challenges in conducting hybrid events. Meticulous planning, extensive testing, and competent technical support are crucial to overcoming these challenges and ensuring a high-quality event experience. By overcoming these technical obstacles, organizers can unlock the full potential of hybrid events, offering both in-person attendees and online participants an enriching and seamless experience.

Engaging virtual participants is one of the most significant challenges in conducting hybrid events. Physical distance can induce a sense of isolation, and the numerous distractions of individual environments can impact the attention and focus of online participants. Therefore, it is crucial for organizers to devise innovative strategies to maximize the engagement and involvement of virtual participants. This chapter discusses methods and best practices that can enhance the engagement of virtual participants in hybrid events.

ENGAGEMENT OF VIRTUAL PARTICIPANTS AS A CENTRAL CHALLENGE

Maintaining the engagement of virtual participants requires organizers to have a profound understanding of the dynamics of digital interactions. Unlike physical participants, who are engaged through the environment and direct interaction with other participants and speakers, virtual participants need targeted incentives to actively participate in the event and engage with the content.

Strategies to Enhance Engagement

1. Interactive Elements: Employing interactive tools such as live polls, Q&A sessions, virtual hand-raising, or chat functions can actively involve virtual participants in the event and create a sense of participation.

2. Networking Opportunities: Virtual networking platforms, such as thematic breakout rooms or one-on-one video calls, offer virtual participants the chance to connect with other attendees and share experiences.

3. Dynamic Content Presentations: The presentation of content should be visually appealing and dynamic to maintain the attention of virtual participants. Incorporating multimedia, such as videos, animations, or interactive presentations, can make the content more vibrant and engaging.

4. Personal Address and Feedback: Directly addressing virtual participants and providing opportunities for feedback contribute to conveying a sense of appreciation and strengthening participant engagement.

Engaging virtual participants is a pivotal challenge in conducting hybrid events. Finding innovative ways to involve this group of participants is crucial for the success of the event. By utilizing interactive elements, offering networking opportunities, presenting content dynamically, and providing a personal touch, organizers can enhance the engagement of virtual participants and create an enriching event experience for all attendees. In an era where virtual event participation is increasingly becoming the norm, these strategies are not only a response to a challenge but also an investment in the future of event design and execution.

Effective content adaptation for two distinct audiences – physical and virtual participants – poses a central challenge in the execution of hybrid events. Creating a coherent, engaging, and accessible experience for both groups requires a nuanced approach in the conceptualization and delivery of event content. This chapter delves into the necessary steps and considerations for tailoring content to both physical and virtual attendees.

CONTENT ADAPTATION AS A KEY ELEMENT OF HYBRID EVENTS

Content adaptation in hybrid events involves more than merely transmitting physical content into the digital realm. It requires acknowledging the specific needs and expectations of both participant groups and designing the content to be equally appealing and interactive for both audiences. This challenging yet crucial task is instrumental in ensuring the quality and success of the event.

Strategies for Successful Content Adaptation

1. Understanding the Audiences: A thorough knowledge of the preferences, behavior, and expectations of both physical and virtual participants is vital for effective content adaptation. Organizers should recognize that the experience and opportunities for interaction differ between the two groups.

2. Differentiated Content Presentation: Content should be curated in a manner that ensures effectiveness in both formats – physical and digital. While physical attendees benefit from the direct atmosphere and interaction, virtual participants require visually appealing and easily accessible content.

3. Interaction Opportunities for Both Audiences: Interaction is a core element of the event experience. Organizers should incorporate mechanisms that enable active participation from both groups, such as integrated polling systems, chat functions, or interactive workshops.

4. Equivalence of Experience: It's crucial that no participant feels secondary. Both physical and virtual attendees should have equal opportunities to engage, ask questions, and benefit from the content.

Adapting content for physical and virtual participants is an essential challenge in conducting hybrid events. Meticulous planning, understanding the target audiences, and differentiated content curation are imperative to create an engaging and enriching event experience for both audiences. By ensuring that all presentations, discussions, and interactions are equally accessible and inclusive for both groups, organizers can maximize the success of their hybrid event and offer a comprehensive and integrative experience.

The integration of digital elements into hybrid events not only opens up new avenues for interaction and reach but also introduces specific security concerns. Particularly, issues related to data protection and data management come to the forefront when participants utilize digital platforms for event participation. This chapter sheds light on the challenges in the realm of security and discusses the significance of comprehensive security measures for the execution of hybrid events.

SECURITY CONCERNS AS A CRITICAL ASPECT OF HYBRID EVENTS

With the incorporation of digital components into events, the risk of data breaches and cyberattacks escalates. Online participation often requires the transmission of personal information, and interaction over digital platforms can expose sensitive data. Ensuring the security of these platforms and the protection of participant data is, therefore, of utmost importance and a central responsibility of the organizers.

Strategies for Ensuring Data Security

1. Secure Platforms: Choosing online platforms that meet high security standards is fundamental. Organizers should opt for providers that implement renowned security protocols and conduct regular security audits.

2. Data Protection Compliance: Adhering to data protection regulations, such as the General Data Protection Regulation (GDPR) in Europe, is crucial. Organizers must ensure that all collected data are protected and that participants are transparently informed about the use of their data.

3. Encryption and Authentication: Implementing encryption technologies for data transmission and introducing authentication procedures for accessing digital content can significantly enhance security.

4. Awareness and Training: Raising awareness among participants and event staff about security risks and the handling of personal data is critical. Training and clear guidelines can help to heighten awareness and promote preventive measures.

Security concerns are an essential aspect of conducting hybrid events. The integration of digital elements necessitates a comprehensive engagement with data protection and data management. By selecting secure platforms, adhering to data protection regulations, implementing encryption and authentication, and promoting awareness and training, organizers can ensure the security of their events and strengthen the trust of participants. In an era where digital interactions are becoming increasingly important, the security of data and platforms is not only a challenge but also a crucial factor in the success and credibility of hybrid events.

Executing hybrid events not only presents logistical and technological challenges for organizers but also necessitates meticulous budget planning and management. The initial investments in technology, platforms, and specialized personnel can be substantial. Therefore, prudent cost management is crucial to ensure the financial viability and success of hybrid events. This chapter addresses the challenges of cost management in hybrid events and discusses approaches for efficient budgeting and cost control.

COST MANAGEMENT AS A CRITICAL COMPONENT OF HYBRID EVENTS

The amalgamation of physical and digital event components results in a complex cost structure. In addition to the usual expenses for physical event organization, additional expenditures for digital platforms, streaming services, technical equipment, and IT support are incurred. To avoid financial strain, thoughtful cost management is imperative.

Strategies for Efficient Cost Management

1. Detailed Budgeting: Precise calculation of all expected costs is the first step towards efficient cost management. This encompasses both the direct costs for location, catering, and personnel, as well as the indirect costs for technology, platforms, and licensing fees.

2. Cost-Benefit Analysis: Assessing the investments in relation to the expected added value of the hybrid event is crucial. This includes considering how the digital component contributes to expanding reach, enhancing participant experience, or improving event efficiency.

3. Selection of Cost-Effective Solutions: Choosing technologies and platforms should take the price-performance ratio into account. Additionally, partnerships with technology providers or sponsorship models can be a way to reduce costs.

4. Scalable Solutions: Especially for organizers who regularly plan hybrid events, investing in scalable solutions can save costs in the long term. Modularly structured platforms and technologies that can adapt to different event sizes and formats offer flexibility and cost efficiency.

Cost management is a pivotal challenge in conducting hybrid events. Additional investments in technology and expertise require precise budgeting and careful cost-benefit analysis.

By selecting cost-effective solutions, considering scalability, and meticulously planning all expenditures, organizers can ensure the financial feasibility of their hybrid events. Efficient cost management significantly contributes to the success of hybrid events and enables organizers to fully exploit the benefits of this innovative event format.

Assessing the success and impact of a hybrid event presents unique challenges for organizers. The complexity of this event format, encompassing both physical and virtual components, necessitates a nuanced consideration and analysis of various success criteria. This chapter introduces approaches and methods to effectively measure and analyze participant satisfaction, engagement, and the Return on Investment (ROI) of hybrid events.

MEASURING SUCCESS AS A CHALLENGE IN HYBRID EVENTS

The assessment of hybrid events is intricate, incorporating the evaluation of both physical and virtual event components. While direct observation and personal feedback from participants are key indicators for physical events, virtual components require an analysis of digital interactions and participant responses. A comprehensive success measurement must, therefore, take into account both aspects and amalgamate them into a holistic assessment.

Strategies for Effective Success Measurement

1. Defining Clear Success Criteria: Prior to the event, clear objectives and success criteria should be established. These might include aspects such as participant numbers, engagement rates, satisfaction scores, or business contacts made.

2. Utilizing Survey and Feedback Tools: Surveys and feedback forms should be deployed for both physical and virtual participants to gather direct feedback on various aspects of the event. Modern event platforms often offer integrated survey functionalities that enable simple and efficient data collection.

3. Analyzing Digital Interaction Data: For the virtual components of the event, analyzing digital interaction data is crucial. Platforms frequently provide detailed statistics on user behavior, participation duration, interaction rates, and more.

4. Calculating the Return on Investment (ROI): Calculating the ROI involves a comprehensive consideration of the costs and benefits generated by the event. In addition to direct revenues, qualitative factors such as brand enhancement, network expansion, or knowledge gains should also be accounted for.

Measuring the success and impact of a hybrid event requires careful planning, the implementation of effective analysis tools, and a holistic view of the event components. By combining quantitative and qualitative assessment methods, organizers can gain a comprehensive understanding of event success and derive valuable insights for optimizing future events. In an era where hybrid events are playing an increasingly important role in the MICE industry, effective success measurement is crucial to fully realize the potential of this innovative event format and to continuously improve it.

Overcoming these challenges necessitates innovative solutions, expertise, and constant adaptation to the evolving needs of participants and technological possibilities. With meticulous planning and a focus on quality and participant experience, however, hybrid events can be successfully executed, creating lasting value for all stakeholders.

CHALLENGES OF HYBRID EVENTS

Hybrid events, a synthesis of real and virtual gatherings, offer unique opportunities for expanding participant reach and providing flexible attendance options. However, they also come with specific challenges that must be carefully addressed to ensure the effectiveness and success of the event format.

A primary issue in implementing hybrid events is the inherent complexity associated with organizing both physical and digital components concurrently. The technical infrastructure must cater not only to the needs of on-site attendees but also to those participating virtually. This demands extensive planning, specialized technical equipment, and competent management throughout the event. The amalgamation of these requirements can lead to increased costs and places high demands on the organizational and coordination team.

Furthermore, the option to choose between physical and virtual participation creates a decision-making situation for attendees. This can lead to a fragmentation of the audience, with one of the formats invariably being less frequented than the other. This disparity can undermine the original intention and dynamics of the event, leading to suboptimal utilization of resources and capacities.

Another drawback is the potential quality discrepancy between the real and virtual experiences. While physical participants benefit from the immediate presence, direct exchange, and atmospheric density of the real event, creating an equivalent and engaging experience for virtual participants can be challenging. Despite advances in technology, virtual interaction can only partially replicate the nuances and engagement of personal interaction. This discrepancy can lead to unequal perceptions and evaluations of the event by different participant groups.

Finally, transforming an originally purely physical event into a hybrid format poses a strategic challenge. The original decision for a real event was based on specific goals and premises that may not be fully compatible with a hybrid format. Transferring the objectives and content from one format to another is not always seamless and can impair the effectiveness of communication and participant engagement. This is akin to translating cinema advertising to radio – the strengths and peculiarities of the original medium do not always translate without losses into another context.

Overall, hybrid events require a careful weighing of the aforementioned disadvantages against the potential benefits. Successful implementation hinges on precise goal definition, thoughtful planning, and a sensitive balance between the expectations and needs of all participant groups.

The essence of a successful hybrid event lies in its duality. It must be meticulously crafted to ensure that both on-site attendees and virtual viewers receive a fully integrated experience. For those present on-site, the event offers the tangible, sensory experiences associated with physical attendance – the opportunity to network face-to-face, interact in real time with speakers, and engage with the surroundings. Conversely, online participants enjoy the convenience and accessibility of participating from any location, utilizing digital tools and platforms to interact, network, and join sessions, almost as if they were personally present.

This duality is what sets hybrid events apart. They are not merely a physical event with an added live stream as an afterthought, nor are they a virtual event with a physical venue. Instead, hybrid events are meticulously designed to ensure that both audiences are not only included but also actively engaged, with each element of the event tailored to meet the unique needs and opportunities of the dual format. To optimize the experience for both audiences, excellent concepts are required for both the online and on-site events. This necessitates sufficient financial resources. The assumption that hybrid events are cheaper is, therefore, incorrect.

THE ESSENCE OF THE MICE INDUSTRY: THE SIGNIFICANCE OF GENUINE ENCOUNTERS AND THE CHALLENGES OF HYBRID EVENTS

The MICE industry is fundamentally about authentic, personal encounters, often framed by high emotionality. Despite technological progress and the introduction of innovative solutions, no virtual alternative has yet fully replicated the essence and value of real encounters. This is primarily because virtual events, despite employing similar terminology, are fundamentally different in nature and impact from real events.

NUMEROUS CHALLENGES IN HYBRID EVENTS

The concept of hybrid events, a symbiosis of real events and their digital presentation, theoretically appears as an advanced solution to offer participants a flexible choice between physical and virtual attendance. However, a more in-depth examination reveals a complex web of challenges and nuances that must be navigated to fully harness the potential of this event format. The hybridization of events should be critically examined, outlining a path whereby the digital aspect can complement the value of the real event without compromising its core characteristics.

Real events are conducted for specific reasons and with clearly defined objectives. They are meticulously crafted communication channels that, due to their physical nature, possess certain strengths such as the intensity of personal encounters and the depth of direct exchange. It is because of these unique strengths that this communication channel was chosen. However, the introduction of the hybrid format may lead to a dilution of these strengths. The decision for the mode of participation may then be based less on content requirements or the desire for intensive exchange and more on factors such as convenience or availability. This could result in the true potential and value of real encounters not being fully realized. It questions the decision made 'pro event' and introduces an online alternative to the event, where it cannot be ruled out that this will ultimately prevail over the offline event because the participants have voted with their feet and a majority opts for online participation. In that case, the original offline event would have abolished itself through hybridization.

THE VALUE OF THE HYBRID APPROACH AS A COMPLEMENTARY ELEMENT

To effectively harness the strengths of hybrid events, it is crucial to view the online part not as a replacement but as a meaningful and strategic complement to the real event. The digital aspect should aim to enhance the value of the real event by fulfilling specific functions that extend beyond the capabilities of a purely physical event. Hybrid, in the sense of pre- and post-event online activities surrounding the actual real (main) event, offers a unique platform to combine the advantages of digital technologies with the immediacy and intensity of physical meetings.

The challenge lies in integrating both formats meaningfully, enriching the experience for all participants. Digital content can be strategically used to maximize engagement and productivity at events.

1. Knowledge Alignment through Digital Content

Knowledge alignment is a crucial aspect to make optimal use of time during the physical part of the event. By providing digital content before the event, organizers can ensure that all participants have a basic understanding of the core topics. This can be achieved through online courses, webinars, or interactive learning modules.

The benefits of this approach are manifold:

- Efficient Use of Time: Aligning the level of knowledge allows participants to focus on in-depth discussions and the exchange of ideas during the event, rather than working through basic content.

- Increased Engagement Rate: Participants introduced to the subject matter in advance are more likely to actively participate in the discourse and contribute their own ideas and questions.

- Personalized Learning Experience: Digital learning content can be tailored to the individual needs of the participants, enhancing the effectiveness of the learning process.

By thoughtfully integrating digital and physical components, hybrid events can offer a comprehensive and inclusive experience. This approach not only leverages the strengths of both formats but also addresses the challenges of hybrid events, ensuring that the true potential and value of real encounters are fully realized. The aim is to create an event experience that is not only adaptable and resilient but also rich in content and engagement, catering to the needs and preferences of a diverse participant base.

2. Dissemination of Key Information in the Online Segment

The online segment of a hybrid event is ideally suited for conveying fundamental information. This strategic division of content allows the physical event to focus on elements that benefit from personal presence: networking, interactive workshops, or panel discussions.

The clear separation of informational delivery and interactive elements offers several advantages:

- Targeted Agenda: Concentrating the physical event on interactive and networking-oriented activities leads to a more dynamic and engaging event.

- Flexible Access to Information: Digital content can be accessed by participants at any time and at their own pace, accommodating various schedules and learning styles.

- Enhanced Preparation: By providing key information beforehand, participants can enter discussions and workshops better prepared, facilitating more profound and productive interactions.

This approach maximizes the strengths of both the physical and virtual components of a hybrid event. It allows for a more structured and participant-focused event, ensuring that each segment – whether online or on-site – delivers its content most effectively and impactfully. This strategic content division not only improves the overall participant experience but also contributes to the tangible outcomes and success of the event. By adopting this dual-focused approach, organizers can create a hybrid event that not only meets but exceeds the expectations of a diverse and discerning audience, setting a new standard in the MICE industry for excellence and innovation.

3. Preparation of Working Groups in Virtual Spaces

Facilitating the formation of small working groups prior to the event offers the opportunity to discuss and prepare specific topics. These virtual meetings enable participants to get acquainted before the physical event, exchange ideas, and collaborate on joint projects.

Active preparation in small groups has several positive effects:

- Active Participation: Early involvement in the subject matter and collaboration in groups fosters engagement and active participation among attendees.

- More Effective Use of the Event: Preliminary work in the groups enables a more focused and targeted discussion during the physical part of the event.

- Strengthening of Networks: Collaboration in small groups enhances relationship building and networking, which can persist beyond the event itself.

Crucial is the meticulous planning and structuring of the digital and physical components of hybrid events to create an enriching and productive event experience for all participants. Through targeted knowledge alignment, effective dissemination of key information, and active preparation of working groups, hybrid events can unfold their full potential and provide a platform for intensive exchange, learning, and networking.

Hybrid events offer tremendous potential, yet their successful execution demands a nuanced approach and a deep understanding of the strengths and weaknesses of both formats. The challenge lies in designing the online segment in such a way that it complements and enriches the value of the real event without diminishing its essence and the power of personal encounters. Through careful planning and strategic utilization of digital components, such events can become a rewarding and valuable addition to the event landscape, offering participants a holistic and multifaceted experience: 365 days a year, 24/7.

THE ROLE OF EVENTS IN THE CORPORATE COMMUNICATION MIX

In the multifaceted realm of corporate communication, events occupy a central and multifunctional position. They serve not only as an effective tool for direct communication but also as a powerful platform for marketing, employee engagement, customer acquisition, and brand building. This section sheds light on the diverse benefits of events and explores why and in what contexts companies strategically integrate them into their communication mix.

DIVERSE ADVANTAGES OF EVENTS IN A BUSINESS CONTEXT

In a world increasingly dominated by digital communication, events retain their unparalleled significance. They offer a platform for direct, personal interactions and open up a myriad of opportunities that companies can leverage to meet and exceed their objectives. This chapter illuminates the multifaceted benefits of events and their role in corporate strategy.

Events stand out in the digital age for their ability to facilitate genuine, face-to-face engagement, forging connections that are often more profound and enduring than those formed through virtual channels. They provide an immersive experience that can captivate the senses, evoke emotions, and create memorable moments, forging a lasting impact on attendees.

Moreover, events offer a unique opportunity for companies to showcase their products, services, and brand personality in a dynamic and interactive environment. They can be tailored to reflect the company's values, culture, and vision, providing a tangible representation of the brand and reinforcing its position in the market.

In addition, events serve as a strategic tool for gathering insights and feedback directly from the target audience, enabling companies to refine their offerings and strategies based on real-time input. The immediacy of the interaction allows for a deeper understanding of customer needs, preferences, and behaviors, contributing to more informed decision-making.

In summary, events are an indispensable component of the corporate communication mix, offering unparalleled opportunities for direct engagement, brand reinforcement, and market intelligence. Their multifaceted benefits make them a strategic asset for any company looking to strengthen its presence, deepen its customer relationships, and drive its business forward in a competitive landscape.

NETWORKING AND SOCIAL INTERACTIONS: THE CORE OF BUSINESS RELATIONSHIPS

In the business world, networking and social interactions are not just valuable; they are often crucial elements for success. Events provide an ideal platform for this purpose. Within the framework of conferences, trade fairs, or informal gatherings, business partners, clients, and colleagues can interact on a personal level. These personal encounters create an atmosphere of trust and mutual appreciation, which is challenging to achieve through digital communication channels.

Personal Exchange as the Cornerstone of Business Success

The personal exchange that occurs at events goes far beyond the mere exchange of business cards. It involves a complex process of listening, sharing stories and experiences, and building sympathies and shared interests. These interactions lay the foundation for solid business relationships. In B2B marketing, such relationships are particularly valuable as decision-making processes are often lengthy and based on trust.

Networking as an Opportunity for Diversification and Innovation

Furthermore, networking events offer an excellent opportunity for the diversification of business relationships. New contacts can bring fresh perspectives and ideas into a company, leading to innovation and improvement. The diversity of participants at events promotes the exchange of cross-industry knowledge and experiences, which in turn lays the groundwork for creative solutions and collaborations.

Long-Term Bonds and Their Value for Companies

Relationships formed at events are often of a long-term nature. A successful event can be the beginning of a business relationship that lasts for years. These long-term bonds are invaluable for companies. They foster stability, open opportunities for joint projects, and can provide valuable support even in challenging times.

Networking and social interactions that occur at events are more than just a pleasant part of business life. They are an essential component of building and maintaining business relationships, crucial for the success of any company. The uniqueness of personal exchange, the potential for diversification and innovation, and the establishment of long-term bonds make networking events an indispensable tool in everyday business. Companies that recognize the importance of these interactions and actively foster them are taking a significant step towards growth and success.

EDUCATION AND LEARNING: THE FOUNDATION FOR EXPERTISE AND LEADERSHIP

Education and learning are pivotal pillars in the realm of professional development and corporate growth. Through conferences, seminars, and workshops held under the umbrella of events, companies unlock extraordinary opportunities to impart and share knowledge. These interactive educational formats offer much more than mere information exchange – they are a key factor in building reputation, demonstrating expertise, and reinforcing industry presence.

Positioning as Thought Leaders

In an increasingly competitive world, being perceived as an authority in one's field is crucial. By offering high-quality educational events, companies position themselves as thought leaders in their industry. This role as a source of knowledge and innovator not only garners attention but also establishes the company as a trusted advisor and preferred partner in its domain.

Knowledge Dissemination as Added Value

Providing educational content and creating learning opportunities is an invaluable added value for clients and partners. Workshops that impart practical skills or seminars offering deep insights into current industry trends are not just a service to clients but also strengthen the relationship between the company and participants. This educational approach fosters long-term bonds and boosts customer loyalty.

Credibility Through Expertise

Sharing expertise and best practices through events underscores a company's competence and credibility. Attendees of such events recognize the value of the presented content and directly associate this expertise with the hosting company. This perceived expertise is a powerful tool for enhancing brand identity and differentiating from competitors.

Visibility and Networking Effects

Educational events not only provide the opportunity to share knowledge but also to gain visibility and build a network. Participants who take away valuable insights and knowledge from an event are likely to share their positive experiences. This networking effect can broaden a company's reach and open up unexpected opportunities for collaborations and business.

Education and learning through events are fundamental strategies for companies aiming to establish themselves as leading forces in their industry. By serving as platforms for knowledge dissemination and exchange, they enhance credibility, foster customer engagement, and increase a company's visibility. Companies investing in education and learning are not just building knowledge; they are building relationships – an investment that pays off in trust, loyalty, and business growth.

MARKETING AND BRANDING: THE ART OF CREATING LASTING IMPRESSIONS AND BRAND EXPERIENCES

In the dynamic world of marketing and branding, events are an irreplaceable tool for leaving lasting impressions and forging a deep emotional connection with the brand. Product launches and brand events are not just platforms for presentations but also for experiences that convey corporate messages in innovative and memorable ways. This section highlights the central role of events in marketing and branding and how they shape the perception and relationship with the brand.

Creativity in Message Delivery

In an era where consumers are bombarded with a plethora of information daily, creative delivery of messages is crucial to capture attention. Events offer a unique stage to present messages innovatively. Through tailored experiences, interactive presentations, and thematically designed events, companies can convey their core messages in a manner that resonates and captivates the audience.

Presentation of Products and Services

Product launches at events are much more than mere demonstrations of new products. They are opportunities to showcase products in action, make their benefits tangible, and narrate the story behind the product. This type of presentation allows participants to develop a deeper connection with the product and understand its value on a personal level.

Creation of Brand Experiences

Brand events are a powerful tool to create unique and unforgettable brand experiences. Through carefully curated experiences, companies can foster an emotional attachment to their brand. Whether through interactive experience stations, immersive technology, or emotional storytelling, brand events can bring corporate values to life and generate lasting emotional resonance among participants.

Strengthening Customer Engagement and Brand Loyalty

Direct interaction with the brand at events plays a pivotal role in strengthening customer engagement. Personal experiences and the opportunity to engage directly with the brand make customers feel valued and understood. These positive experiences promote brand loyalty and can lead customers to become brand ambassadors, sharing their positive experiences and recommending the brand within their network.

Marketing and branding through events are an art form aimed at leaving lasting impressions and creating a deep connection with the brand. By crafting unique brand experiences and creatively presenting products, companies can build an emotional bond with their customers that extends beyond the moment. Direct interaction and immersive experiences at events strengthen customer engagement, enhance brand loyalty, and position the brand in the hearts and minds of customers. In a world where differentiation and emotional connection are paramount, events offer an unparalleled platform to bring the brand to life and achieve lasting impact.

MOTIVATION AND TEAMBUILDING: CATALYSTS FOR A STRONG CORPORATE CULTURE

In an era where corporate culture and employee well-being are increasingly in the spotlight, internal events such as company retreats and team-building activities are gaining significance. They are not merely occasions to break from routine, but also serve as powerful tools to bolster employee morale, enhance internal communication, and foster a vibrant team spirit. This section explores the multifaceted role of motivation and team-building events at the heart of corporate culture.

Strengthening Employee Morale and Engagement

Events focused on motivation and team-building significantly contribute to employee satisfaction and engagement. Shared experiences and activities cultivate a sense of belonging and mutual respect. This sense of community is crucial to maintain motivation and create a work environment where every individual feels valued and understood.

Enhancing Internal Communication

Communication is the backbone of any successful organization. Team-building events offer a unique platform to break down barriers and promote open, honest communication channels. Cooperative tasks and interactive challenges encourage team members to freely express their thoughts and ideas, leading to a more transparent and effective communication culture.

Promoting Team Spirit and Collaboration

Collaboration within a team often comes with challenges, especially in large or diversified companies. Team-building events help cultivate a strong team spirit by highlighting the individual strengths of each member while emphasizing the value of collective effort. Joint activities and challenges foster cohesion and mutual support, creating an environment where collaboration and collective success flourish.

Creating a Positive and Productive Corporate Culture

A positive corporate culture is a critical factor for business success. Motivation and team-building events contribute significantly to creating and maintaining such a culture. They demonstrate to employees that their welfare and development are priorities. Investments in such events send a clear message from the company to its staff that their contributions are valued and that their satisfaction and well-being are of paramount importance.

Motivation and team-building are more than just buzzwords in the modern business world; they are vital components of a thriving corporate culture. Internal events geared towards these aspects play a crucial role in enhancing employee morale, improving internal communication, fostering team spirit, and creating a positive and productive work environment. Companies that invest in such events not only show appreciation towards their employees but also lay the groundwork for sustained success and growth.

FUNDRAISING AND AWARENESS-RAISING: THE CORNERSTONE OF CHARITABLE MISSIONS

In the world of nonprofit organizations, events stand as an indispensable pillar, not only as a means for fundraising but also as powerful instruments for awareness-raising and mobilizing support. These gatherings often serve as the nexus where passionate individuals, committed donors, and the broader public unite to collectively instigate positive change. This section delves into the profound significance of fundraising and awareness-raising events and their immeasurable value to charitable organizations.

Mobilizing Support and Resources

Fundraising events are pivotal moments where nonprofit organizations garner the necessary financial resources to propel their projects and initiatives. Spanning gala dinners, benefit concerts, or charity runs, these events provide a platform where organizations can showcase the fruits of their labor and highlight the urgent necessity of their mission. Through direct interaction with attendees, they foster a deeper understanding of their goals and encourage a willingness to support.

Awareness-Raising and Public Relations

Beyond fundraising, events play a central role in raising awareness and public relations. They offer nonprofits the opportunity to disseminate their messages widely and reach a broader audience. Through informative presentations, inspiring speeches, and showcasing success stories, they can accentuate the importance of their work and sharpen awareness for the issues they address.

Networking and Community Building

Events also serve as a hub for networking and community building. They bring together like-minded individuals, facilitate exchanges among those committed to similar causes, and create a robust network of supporters. These communities are indispensable, forming the backbone of support that nonprofits need to be successful in the long term.

Strengthening Donor Relationships

Direct interaction with donors and supporters at events is an invaluable part of donor stewardship. By expressing their appreciation and maintaining personal contact, organizations strengthen their ties with benefactors. These relationships are invaluable, securing continuous support and long-term engagement from donors.

Fundraising and awareness-raising events are much more than mere means to resource acquisition; they are potent tools enabling nonprofit organizations to advance their missions, raise awareness for critical issues, build strong communities, and maintain enduring relationships with their supporters. Through the direct engagement these events facilitate, organizations can effectively broadcast their messages, mobilize the necessary resources, and generate a wave of support and awareness that extends far beyond the event itself.

ENTERTAINMENT AND LEISURE: CULTURAL ENRICHMENT AND BRAND STRENGTHENING

In a world increasingly dominated by work and productivity, entertainment and leisure provide a valuable counterbalance and enrich social and cultural life. Cultural events, concerts, and festivals play a pivotal role in this regard. They are not just a source of joy and relaxation but also have the potential to strengthen community bonds, foster cultural understanding, and uniquely shape the image of brands and companies. This section illuminates the multifaceted importance of events in the realms of entertainment and leisure and their impact on quality of life and brand perception.

Enriching Quality of Life through Culture and Entertainment

Cultural events, concerts, and festivals offer individuals the opportunity to break from the routine and immerse themselves in the world of art and entertainment. These events are more than mere distractions; they are an enrichment to the quality of life. They enable participants to discover new perspectives, find inspiration, and connect with others over shared interests. In an increasingly interconnected world, such events provide a space for genuine, immediate experiences.

Strengthening Community and Promoting Cultural Understanding

Entertainment and leisure events have the unique ability to bring together people from diverse backgrounds. They promote cultural understanding and acceptance by opening a window to different ways of life and traditions. Through the shared experience of art and culture, these events strengthen community cohesion and build bridges between diverse social and cultural groups.

Brand Strengthening through Association with Positive Experiences

For brands and companies, cultural events, concerts, and festivals offer a unique opportunity to enhance their image and be associated with positive experiences. Association with high-quality events can significantly improve the perception of a brand. Companies that sponsor or host such events demonstrate their commitment to culture and community and benefit from the positive resonance these events evoke.

Entertainment and leisure through cultural events, concerts, and festivals are an indispensable part of a livable society. They not only provide a platform for relaxation and enjoyment but also foster cultural understanding, strengthen community bonds, and offer brands and companies the chance to positively and sustainably shape their image. By investing in such events, companies contribute to cultural diversity, enrich the quality of life, and simultaneously strengthen their market position. In a world where authenticity and social engagement are increasingly important, entertainment and leisure through cultural events are a key element for success and societal recognition.

INNOVATION AND INSPIRATION: CRUCIBLES OF FUTURE VISIONS

In a world characterized by rapid changes and continuous innovations, trade fairs and exhibitions are not just events but actual epicenters of innovation and inspiration. They serve as vibrant forums where companies and individuals converge to shape and experience the future. This section delves into the role of trade fairs and exhibitions as platforms for showcasing innovations and as sources of inspiration for new ideas and trends.

Presentation Stage for Companies

For businesses, trade fairs and exhibitions present a unique opportunity to showcase their latest innovations, products, and services to a broad and often international audience. These events provide a stage where companies can not only present their latest developments but also communicate their visions and values. Participating in such events underscores a company's commitment to innovation and quality and reinforces its position as a leading force in the industry.

Source of Inspiration for Attendees

For attendees, trade fairs and exhibitions are much more than showcases of technological advancements and product launches. They are places of inspiration, where individuals have the opportunity to discover the latest trends, engage with innovative concepts, and draw inspiration from creative solutions and ideas. Direct access to the latest developments and interaction with the minds behind the innovations make these events an inexhaustible source of inspiration.

Collaboration and Networking

Trade fairs and exhibitions not only facilitate the exchange of ideas but also provide a platform for collaboration and networking. Companies, industry experts, researchers, and innovators come together to forge partnerships, initiate collaborations, and collectively address the challenges of the future. These collaborations often mark the beginning of long-term projects and partnerships that extend far beyond the duration of the event.

Market Research and Competitive Analysis

In addition to showcasing innovations, trade fairs and exhibitions also offer companies the opportunity to conduct market research and competitive analysis. By observing industry trends, analyzing competitor products, and gathering feedback, companies can gain valuable insights that contribute to the further development of their products and strategies.

Innovation and inspiration are the driving forces behind trade fairs and exhibitions. These events are not just platforms for presenting new products and services but also venues where the future is visionary shaped. They offer companies a stage to position themselves as leaders in innovation and provide visitors with a source of inspiration and learning. By fostering collaboration, networking, and competitive analysis, trade fairs and exhibitions play a central role in the dynamic world of innovation and significantly contribute to the progress and success of companies and industries.

FEEDBACK AND MARKET RESEARCH: A WINDOW INTO CUSTOMER PERSPECTIVE AND MARKET DYNAMICS

In today's fast-paced business world, the ability to respond to customer feedback and understand market shifts is crucial for a company's long-term success. Events offer an invaluable platform to gather direct feedback from customers, partners, and industry peers. This immediate feedback enables companies to refine their products, services, and strategies, aligning them with market needs and expectations. This section discusses the importance of feedback and market research within the context of events and how they contribute to strategic decision-making.

Direct Feedback: The Key to Customer Engagement and Product Enhancement

Events provide an ideal opportunity to receive direct feedback from the most crucial stakeholders – the customers. Through product demonstrations, workshops, and Q&A sessions, companies can collect immediate responses to their offerings. This feedback is invaluable as it provides insights into the strengths and weaknesses of products and indicates how they can be improved. Companies that take this feedback seriously and act upon it demonstrate to their customers that their opinions are valued, thereby increasing customer loyalty and satisfaction.

Market Research: Insight into Trends and Preferences

Events are also an excellent means for market research. They offer companies the chance to observe industry trends, conduct competitive analysis, and gain insights into the evolving preferences and behaviors of customers. By interacting with a wide range of participants, companies can collect and analyze data crucial for the development of future strategies and products.

Strategy Adjustment: Flexible and Market-Oriented

The information gathered at events is a powerful tool for strategic planning. Companies that recognize the importance of feedback and market research and use this information are better positioned to dynamically adjust their strategies and make market-oriented decisions. Whether it's launching a new product, tweaking a marketing campaign, or developing an innovative service, insights from events can make the difference between success and failure.

Feedback and market research are pivotal elements of any successful business strategy. Events provide a unique platform to gather valuable feedback, understand market trends, and make strategic decisions. Companies that seize these opportunities position themselves as customer-focused and market-aware. By integrating insights gained from events into their business processes and decisions, they can better meet the needs and expectations of their customers and maintain a competitive edge in a rapidly changing market environment.

Events are a versatile and potent instrument in any company's arsenal. They offer a platform for direct interaction, education, marketing, team-building, fundraising, entertainment, innovation, and market research. Through strategic use of events, companies can strengthen their brands, deepen customer relationships, motivate employees, launch new products, and thrive in a constantly evolving market landscape. However, effectively integrating events into corporate strategy requires careful planning, a clear understanding of business objectives, and a deep knowledge of the target audience. When these aspects are considered, events can become a powerful tool for corporate growth and success.

THE ROLE OF EVENTS IN THE COMMUNICATION MIX: A STRATEGIC PERSPECTIVE

Incorporating events into a company's communication mix is a strategic decision with far-reaching implications for brand image, customer relationships, and business development. Offering a dynamic platform for interaction and presentation, events can be a crucial factor for corporate success when utilized correctly. This chapter sheds light on the various reasons and timings for companies to integrate events into their communication mix and demonstrates how these can be strategically leveraged to meet specific corporate objectives.

1. Product Launches: The Starting Point for Market Success

Product launches are critical moments in a product's lifecycle. Organizing events allows companies not only to impressively present their new products but also to attract media and public interest. These occasions are an opportunity to highlight the uniqueness and utility of the product and act as a launchpad for market success. A successful product launch can capture the attention of potential customers, elevate brand awareness, and lay a solid foundation for future sales successes.

2. Brand Building and Positioning: Standing Out from the Crowd

Events are a potent instrument for strengthening a company's brand building and positioning. Through meticulously conceived events, companies can express their brand identity, build emotional connections with their audience, and clearly differentiate themselves from the competition. Events offer a unique opportunity to make brand values tangible, communicate brand messages, and establish profound relationships with the audience.

3. Customer Retention: Strengthening Relationships

Maintaining existing customers is just as crucial for companies as acquiring new ones. Customer-specific events such as appreciation gatherings, exclusive product demonstrations, or client meetings provide a platform to deepen relationships with customers and foster loyalty. Through these personal encounters, companies can express their appreciation for their customers, receive feedback, and lay the groundwork for long-term customer retention.

4. Employee Engagement: Promoting a Positive Work Environment

Events can also be used internally to boost employee engagement and foster a positive corporate culture. Employee events such as team-building activities, company celebrations, or training seminars contribute to improving communication and collaboration within the team, enhancing employee satisfaction, and creating a motivating work environment. Investments in such events signal to employees that the company takes their development and well-being seriously.

5. Building Relationships with Business Partners: Strengthening Networks

Nurturing business relationships is a vital component of corporate success. By organizing or attending industry events, networking events, or partnership meetings, companies can strengthen existing relationships with business partners and initiate new collaborations. These events offer an ideal opportunity to exchange ideas, discuss common goals, and lay the foundation for long-term, successful partnerships.

6. Crisis Management: Creating Trust and Transparency

During times of crisis, events can be an effective tool to regain stakeholder trust, demonstrate transparency, and promote constructive dialogue. Through press conferences, information events, or discussion forums, companies can address concerns, present their perspective, and showcase solutions. Such events can significantly contribute to reinforcing trust in the company and paving the way for positive development.

7. Lead Generation and Sales Support: Unlocking New Business Opportunities

Trade shows, exhibitions, and industry conferences are excellent platforms for lead generation and sales support. By presenting products and services, interacting with potential customers, and participating in industry discussions, companies can identify new business opportunities, receive direct feedback, and strengthen their sales strategies. These events offer an ideal opportunity to showcase product portfolios, understand market needs, and establish valuable business contacts.

8. Market Research: Gaining Insights into the Market

Events offer a unique opportunity to receive direct feedback from customers, partners, and industry peers and gain profound insights into the market. Through product demonstrations, panel discussions, and direct conversations, companies can gather valuable information about market preferences, customer expectations, and industry trends. These insights are invaluable for strategic planning, product development, and market positioning. By utilizing insights gathered at events, companies can refine their offerings, adjust their strategies, and enhance their competitiveness.

Integrating events into a company's communication mix offers a multitude of strategic opportunities to meet and exceed business objectives. Whether it's launching new products, strengthening the brand, engaging customers, motivating employees, nurturing business relationships, managing crises, generating leads, or gaining market insights – events provide a dynamic and interactive platform to achieve these goals. Careful planning and strategic use of events can bolster a company's market position, deepen relationships, and secure sustainable business success.

The decision to integrate an event into the communication mix depends on various factors, such as specific business objectives, industry, product lifecycle, and current market developments. A well-considered event can create significant value at different stages of corporate growth and critical junctures. Events are a versatile and powerful tool in a company's communication mix, enabling direct, personal interaction – an increasingly valuable commodity in our digital era. Strategic planning of events can empower companies to strengthen their brand, deepen customer relationships, motivate employees, launch new products, and navigate successfully in a constantly changing market environment. However, effectively integrating events into the communication mix requires careful planning, clear understanding of business goals, and deep knowledge of the target audience. When these aspects are considered, events can become a mighty tool for corporate growth and success.

MISCONCEPTIONS AND DIFFERING PERSPECTIVES IN THE MICE INDUSTRY

The MICE industry is characterized by two primary perspectives: that of the providers – destinations, venues, hotels, and suppliers – and that of the demand side: corporations, associations, and their intermediaries like event agencies. While event agencies generate revenue through consultancy, conception, planning, organization, and execution of events, many in the industry focus solely on these aspects, leading to a limited viewpoint. This narrow perspective can significantly hinder the ability to recognize and act upon the "bigger picture."

The economic significance of in-person events in the MICE industry cannot be understated. These events act as significant economic engines for cities, municipalities, and countries, serving not just as a direct industry but also shaping the socio-economic fabric of host destinations. The economic impact of these in-person events extends far beyond the immediate stakeholders involved, influencing a wide array of secondary industries.

The economic impetus generated by MICE events is particularly notable in the tourism sector. MICE events draw participants from around the world, temporarily bringing them to a destination, making them a pivotal factor in the tourism sector. Participants of these events – be it conferences, exhibitions, or incentive trips – tend to spend significantly more than average tourists. These increased expenditures reflect not only in the direct costs of participation fees, accommodation, and catering but also in indirect expenses for local services and products. From retail stores to restaurants, to transportation services – the positive economic impact of MICE events permeates numerous sectors of the local economy, contributing to job creation, fostering entrepreneurship, and promoting regional development.

However, it is crucial for stakeholders within the MICE industry to adopt a holistic perspective and recognize the far-reaching economic, social, and cultural implications of their activities. Only through a comprehensive understanding of the complex dynamics and interdependencies within the sector can sustainable strategies be developed that not only ensure the immediate success of the events but also have a long-term positive impact on the involved communities and the overall economic structure.

The MICE industry, encompassing meetings, incentives, conferences, and exhibitions, is not just a driver of direct economic activities but also a catalyst for secondary economic processes that extend well beyond the immediate service providers. These secondary effects, often referred to as the multiplier effect on the local economy, are a pivotal characteristic of the economic significance of MICE events.

MICE events bring increased purchasing power to destinations. Participants of conferences, exhibitions, and other professional gatherings tend to spend substantial amounts during their stay in host cities. These expenditures are not limited to obvious items like venues, accommodations, or event agencies. A broad spectrum of secondary service providers also benefit from this economic activity. Taxi drivers, gastronomy businesses, retailers, and cultural venues experience a direct economic boost as MICE participants avail services and products beyond the actual event. This multiplier effect ensures that the revenues generated by MICE events are recirculated multiple times in the local economy, thus significantly expanding the economic value chain.

In addition to immediate economic stimulation, the regular hosting of MICE events also has long-term positive effects on the sustainable economic development of destinations. The continuous demand for local services and products creates stable income sources, contributing directly to local economic performance. This stability and predictability allow affected communities to make investments in critical areas such as infrastructure, education, culture, and social services. Such investments not only improve the quality of life for residents but also make the destination more attractive for future events and visitors, fostering a positive cycle of economic and social development.

It is, however, important to emphasize that these positive effects are sustainable only when they align with the ecological and social standards of the affected communities. The MICE industry, therefore, faces the challenge of designing its activities in a manner that promotes not only economic but also ecological and social sustainability. This requires careful planning, consideration of the interests of all stakeholders, and continuous assessment of the impacts of the events.

In summary, the MICE industry plays a significant role in the global economy. The industry has the potential to act not only as a direct industry but also as a multiplier, invigorating local economies, creating jobs, and contributing to the sustainable development of destinations. Maximizing these positive effects, however, requires conscious and strategically oriented action from all participants.

MICE events are pivotal drivers of economic and social development for cities and communities. One of the standout features of these events is their ability to significantly boost tax revenues, having far-reaching positive effects on public infrastructure and the common good.

The additional income generated by MICE events flows into local and national budgets in various ways. A significant portion of these revenues comes from taxes levied on the revenues generated by the events. This includes value-added taxes on services and products, income taxes from salaries of those employed in the industry, and other specific levies directly or indirectly associated with the execution of the events. These tax revenues are crucial for public budgets, providing the necessary funds for financing essential public services.

The financing of public services such as schools, hospitals, and security services is significantly supported by the tax revenues generated by MICE events. The enhancement of these facilities not only contributes to strengthening public infrastructure but also promotes the general well-being and quality of life of citizens. Moreover, the additional funds allow investments in projects and programs that promote the common good and advance local development.

In addition to boosting tax revenues, MICE events are also significant employers. They create numerous jobs directly associated with the organization and execution of the events, as well as indirectly in sectors connected to the industry. These jobs span a wide spectrum of qualifications and fields of activity – from highly qualified positions in event planning and management to service professions in gastronomy, transportation, and security. The jobs created by MICE events contribute not only to economic stability by providing income and employment opportunities but also promote social prosperity by offering meaningful activities and developmental prospects to individuals.

In conclusion, MICE events play a crucial role in the economic and social development of destinations. By boosting tax revenues and creating jobs, they significantly contribute to strengthening public infrastructure, promoting the common good, and ensuring social prosperity. Strategic promotion and sustainable development of the MICE industry are therefore essential for the future viability and prosperity of cities and communities.

The economic significance of in-person events in the MICE industry is undeniable. They serve as a vital industry, supporting not only the immediate stakeholders involved but also dynamizing the broader economy, contributing to public funding, strengthening the job market, and contributing to the social and cultural development of host destinations. This wide-ranging economic impact underscores the importance of in-person events and their role as a driving force for growth and prosperity. In-person events sell schnitzel, online events do not, and hybrid events hardly do.

THE COVID-19 PANDEMIC KICK: A STRATEGIC SHIFT IN THE MICE INDUSTRY

The MICE industry underwent a significant transformation during the COVID-19 pandemic. The enforced physical distancing led to a rapid adoption of digital solutions. Stakeholders in the MICE sector, including convention bureaus, hotels, hotel chains, and Destination Management Companies (DMCs), responded swiftly, inviting event planners to pivot towards online events. This shift, often referred to as "The COVID-19 Pandemic Kick," had profound implications on sales strategies within the industry.

In an initial response to the new circumstances, many hotels and other providers heavily invested in their internet infrastructure and set up virtual studios for online and hybrid events. However, upon closer examination, questions arose about the effectiveness of these decisions. Why would event planners book hotel rooms if the hotel simultaneously offers a studio for online events, thus rendering the physical presence of participants redundant? It soon became clear: while online events generate reach, they do not sell hotel rooms, food, beverages, or additional services – in short, online events do not sell "schnitzel"!

The challenge lies not in the use of online communication per se but in how it's employed by MICE providers in their sales and marketing efforts. The core issue is that traditional mechanisms of personal selling and business initiation are often unreflectively transferred into the digital realm, without considering the specifics and demands of the digital space. The traditional sales call, once the backbone of sales efforts, is no longer fitting in a digitally dominated sales environment.

The conventional MICE sales method, premised on the belief that a higher number of appointments leads to more potential business, shows its limitations in an increasingly digital world. The behavior and expectations of the target audience have evolved, yet many in MICE sales seem to overlook this. Significant investments are made to drive target customers to appointments, such as through hosted buyer programs, but a fundamental overhaul of MICE sales is often shied away from. There's a lack of courage and competence to explore new avenues and adapt sales strategies to new realities.

For MICE providers, it's crucial to rethink and adapt their sales strategies. They need to understand the possibilities of the digital world not merely as an extension of traditional sales channels but as an opportunity to fundamentally renew interaction with their target audience. Instead of using digital tools merely as a platform for transmitting well-known sales formats, they should be utilized to create genuine, value-adding interactions. Storytelling, content marketing, and the creation of interactive, value-based experiences are key components in this new approach.

The MICE industry is faced with the challenge of fundamentally rethinking its sales strategies and adapting them to digital realities. This requires a profound understanding of the needs and behaviors of the target audience in the digital world, as well as the courage to question and redesign traditional sales approaches. By doing so, MICE sales can remain successful in an increasingly digitalized world and fully exploit the potentials of the digital space.

THE PANDEMIC PIVOT: HYBRID AND ONLINE EVENTS FROM A MICE PROVIDER'S PERSPECTIVE

Would Amazon confine its products to a closed online event? The answer is a resounding no. Then why, one might ponder, does the MICE Sales sector follow such a path?

In the 21st century's digital world, sales behaviours have transformed profoundly, especially in online retail. Companies like Amazon have demonstrated that successful online sales follow a clear structure: 1. Generating attention, 2. Being considered, 3. Engaging in conversations, and 4. Culminating in a purchase decision. For providers in the MICE sector, particularly in sales, these insights offer significant cues for shaping their online presence and sales strategies.

A critical aspect often overlooked in many MICE suppliers' digital sales strategies is the need to make their products and services accessible to a broader audience. Unlike successful online stores that openly present their products for search engines to find, many MICE suppliers tend to conceal their offerings behind the closed virtual doors of online events. This practice results in a scenario where, apart from a small circle of already involved participants, nobody learns about the products and services on offer. The result is a lack of widespread awareness and the inability for search engines like Google to find and index the content. The simple yet accurate truth remains: "If Google can't find it, it doesn't exist." And if it doesn't exist, it certainly can't be purchased.

Therefore, MICE sales face the challenge of rethinking their digital sales strategies and adapting the mechanisms of successful online sales. This primarily involves making their offerings visible to a wider audience. Rather than organizing closed online events that require registration and logging in, content should be presented openly and accessibly. This approach allows potential customers to discover, learn about, and develop an interest in the offerings.

In today's rapidly evolving digital landscape, it's crucial for MICE sector suppliers to understand and effectively harness the mechanisms of online sales. The ability to capture the attention of potential customers, pique their interest, engage in dialogue with them, and ultimately influence purchasing decisions is fundamental to success in the digital world. This chapter delves deeper into the four stages of the online sales process and explains how MICE suppliers can adapt their strategies to these stages, thereby strengthening their online presence and boosting their sales success.

1. Generating Attention
In the digital world, visibility is key. MICE suppliers must ensure that their offerings are picked up by search engines and easily found by potential customers. Effective search

engine optimization (SEO) is crucial here, involving content optimization with relevant keywords, the cultivation of backlinks, and regular content updates to improve placement in search results. Furthermore, leveraging relevant platforms and social media is important to increase reach and engage the target audience where they reside.

2. Being Considered

Once the attention of potential customers is captured, interest must be fostered through engaging and informative presentations of the offerings. High-quality imagery, compelling descriptions, and clearly communicated unique selling propositions (USPs) are vital to prompt the target audience to delve deeper into the offerings. The presentation should clearly articulate the added value and address the specific needs of the target audience.

3. Engaging in Conversations

Stimulating dialogue and interaction with potential customers is another critical step in the online sales process. Interactive features such as comment sections, live chats, or interactive product presentations can help build a relationship with prospects. Through direct exchange, the specific needs and questions of potential customers can be identified and addressed, reinforcing trust in the brand and the offerings.

4. Culminating in a Purchase Decision

The final step in the online sales process is bringing about the purchase decision. The entire process, from expressing interest to concluding a purchase, should be seamless and enjoyable for the customer. This includes intuitive website navigation, transparent information on prices and conditions, secure payment methods, and reliable customer service.

By carefully tailoring their online presence and sales strategies to these four stages of the online sales process, MICE providers can significantly enhance the visibility of their offerings, reach a broader audience, and boost their sales success in the digital world. The digital presence is not an isolated aspect but must be understood as an integral part of the overall strategy and continuously optimized.

In the digital era, sales in the MICE industry are confronted with new challenges and opportunities. The foundational principles of online sales provide a blueprint for success, yet their implementation requires a deep understanding of the digital landscape and the needs of the target audience. The core elements of this approach are the continuous availability of content, the promotion of communication, and reaching the right target customers. However, in practice, it's evident that many MICE suppliers neglect fundamental aspects in designing their online events and sales strategies.

The conventional practice of showcasing products and services behind the virtual walls of closed online events starkly contrasts the success principles of effective online sales. Products that cannot be found by search engines like Google stand little chance of capturing the target audience's attention. Consequently, the visibility and findability of the offered content are crucial factors for sales success.

In the MICE industry, the importance of suppliers and their products in organizing sales events and exhibitions is often underestimated. While destinations and venues serve as primary attractions for recruiting event planners, the participating exhibitors frequently remain unmentioned. This practice leads to a discrepancy between the expectations of event planners and the actual experience at the events. To overcome this challenge, it's essential for both organizers and suppliers to rethink their communication strategies and focus on presenting the participating suppliers prominently.

The Hybrid Sales concept, as applied by e.g. MICEboard, offers an innovative solution to this issue. In this approach, participating suppliers and their offerings are comprehensively presented well before the event. This transparency allows event planners to make informed decisions about their participation and ensures that expectations for personal appointments are met. Moreover, the online presentation of suppliers on various platforms increases their visibility, thus fostering interest from the target audience and enhancing the potential for business initiation.

MICE suppliers must recognize that while personal contact remains a central element in the sales process, the significance of online presence and communication is steadily increasing. Recent developments underscore that a combination of a strong online presence and targeted personal meetings paves the way for successful business relationships. In an era where digital interactions are gaining increasing importance, MICE suppliers must adapt their sales strategies accordingly to succeed in the digital world and fully exploit the potentials.

ARE ONLINE EVENTS HERE TO STAY, AND DO HYBRID EVENTS TRULY OFFER THE BEST OF BOTH WORLDS?

In the dynamic landscape of the event industry, fundamental questions are gaining prominence in the era of digital transformation, especially in the context of recent global developments. Are online events merely a short-term response to extraordinary circumstances, or do they represent a more enduring shift? Do hybrid events indeed provide the best of both worlds? These questions necessitate a nuanced examination and reflection on the future direction of the event industry.

The Covid-19 pandemic precipitated an unprecedented paradigm shift within the event industry. Prior to this global crisis, the unwavering credo was: "Nothing beats a live event and face-to-face communication." Online and hybrid events, despite the availability of technical solutions, were regarded more as a contingency plan than a genuine alternative by event planners. However, the pandemic-induced restrictions catalysed a fundamental attitudinal shift virtually overnight. The imperative to maintain physical distancing and the prohibition of in-person events left little choice but to embrace digital event formats.

Hybrid events, which combine physical presence with virtual participation, garnered particular attention during this period. The industry adapted swiftly, heralding hybrid events as the optimal synthesis of two realms. These formats promised to integrate the advantages of physical proximity with the capabilities of digital technology. Practically, this meant that event planners deployed their skills and expertise flexibly to accommodate the new realities. They demonstrated adaptability and innovation by actively contributing to the digital transformation of the industry.

Now, in the post-pandemic resurgence phase where in-person events are increasingly feasible, interest in hybrid and online events seems to be waning. Discourse within the industry is shifting again. Authentic, physical encounters are experiencing a renaissance, being heralded as the core of human interaction and an integral component of the event experience. There's talk of an innate "campfire gene" within every individual, symbolising the deep longing for personal interaction and shared experiences.

However, this perspective should not obscure the fact that the industry must continue to rely on flexibility and adaptability. It's anticipated that the preferences and requirements of target audiences will keep evolving rapidly and that external factors, such as health or economic crises, could lead to a realignment. The event industry, therefore, must remain agile, evolving both physical and digital formats to meet a diverse range of needs and to create resilient strategies for the future.

In summary, the future of the event industry lies both in the further development of the physical event experience and in the integration and optimisation of digital and hybrid formats. The industry faces the challenge of finding a balance between the human need for physical proximity and the multifaceted possibilities offered by digital technologies. Only by doing so can it meet changing requirements and remain successful and relevant in the long term.

The Covid-19 pandemic has led to fundamental changes in many sectors of the economy and societal life, particularly noticeable in the world of corporate governance and the MICE industry, where profound shifts are evident. A stark example is the transformation of shareholder meetings of DAX-listed corporations from traditional physical gatherings to digital formats.

The transition to online shareholder meetings was embraced by corporations, offering not just significant cost savings that would have been incurred for organising and conducting a physical event but also enabling them to make the event more efficient. Critical comments from shareholders and unwanted incidents, like the infamous pie-throwing at the board of a car manufacturer, can be regulated and managed more effectively in a digital setting. The shareholder event thus morphs into a sort of 'Boardroom TV,' with corporate management firmly in control of the communication and the event experience.

An interesting aspect of this development is also the coordination of dates for these online events. For instance, in 2023, 30 DAX-listed companies agreed on a common day in May for their shareholder meetings, with four of them even starting their live stream at the same time. Such scheduling presents a significant challenge for professional investors, forced to choose between simultaneous events.

While the benefits for corporations are clear, the implications of this transformation for the MICE industry and local economies are often overlooked. The shift from physical to online events has direct consequences for venues, catering, retail, the hotel industry, and tourism in the regions traditionally hosting these shareholder meetings. The absence of hundreds of participants means significant revenue loss for local service providers and a weakening of the regional economy.

This perspective was almost always overlooked by both corporations and agencies in the transition to online events. The long-term consequences of this development are gradually becoming apparent, highlighting the need to comprehensively reconsider event format decisions and their impact on all stakeholders involved.

It's clear that while the decision for online shareholder meetings is understandable from the corporations' perspective, a holistic view of the impact on the MICE industry and local economies is essential. It's crucial to find a balanced relationship between the benefits of digital formats and the preservation of the interests of local service providers and the regional economy, to promote a sustainable and future-proof event culture.

In recent years, the MICE industry has faced unprecedented challenges. The Covid-19 pandemic has not only transformed society as a whole but has also fundamentally altered the structure and dynamics of the event and hospitality sectors. The questions now arising are complex and demand an in-depth exploration of the causal relationships and the resulting consequences for the industry.

By 2022, approximately 36,000 hospitality businesses in Germany had to shut their doors, with more closures occurring weekly. The pandemic radically shifted the perspectives of event planners, often leading to a sense of directionlessness. This situation resulted in a significant exodus of professionals from the industry, some voluntarily, others forced out by layoffs. However, it would be simplistic to attribute these developments solely to the pandemic. The truth is more complex, revealing fundamental structural changes within the event industry.

The shift towards online and hybrid events during the pandemic has demonstrated that the traditional skills of an event project manager are not necessarily required for organizing and conducting such events. This also applies to personnel in restaurants, hotels, or event venues. Bookings for physical events declined, along with the demand for associated services. This shift has triggered a chain of reactions with lasting effects on the industry's infrastructure. The infrastructure necessary for conducting physical events is now significantly reduced and simultaneously more expensive. This has led to increased costs for physical events, a development that both clients and service providers must understand and accept.

Concurrently, the pandemic has accelerated a trend towards online alternatives. About 50% of business travel, compared to 2018, has been discontinued and replaced with online video calls. While this shift has negative impacts on certain sectors of the economy, it also holds positive implications for the climate. In this tension between sustainability and economic viability, a new path is emerging: the need to find a balance between indispensable live events and effective online and hybrid alternatives.

The MICE industry thus stands at a crossroads. The question is no longer merely whether online or hybrid events are here to stay. Rather, it's about the necessity to find a new equilibrium that meets the changed conditions and requirements. This requires not just an adaptation of business models and a realignment of competencies but also a new mindset that considers economic, social, and ecological aspects. The industry must reinvent itself to remain sustainably successful and relevant in a world where "video calls don't sell schnitzels."

The swift adoption of online and hybrid events in the MICE industry during and after the Covid-19 pandemic has fundamentally altered the event landscape. Numerous industry suppliers, including hotels and event agencies, quickly responded to the new circumstances by integrating digital components into their services. This step, initially driven by the need to adapt to pandemic-related restrictions, has had unforeseen consequences and now presents providers with complex challenges.

Hotels that established studios for hybrid and online events within their facilities found that while this investment opened up new possibilities on one hand, it undermined the core competencies of their business model - selling rooms and catering to participants - on the other. By promoting event formats that reduce or even eliminate the need for physical presence, they paradoxically diminished their own demand.

Event agencies, traditionally reliant on the power of live events and direct communication, suddenly found themselves cast in the role of online event experts. This repositioning, initially intended as an adjustment to new market conditions, inadvertently weakened their position for the post-pandemic era. Without a long-term strategy and awareness of the lasting impacts of this realignment, they unintentionally undermined their infrastructure for onsite events.

Pandemics, economic crises, terrorism, and climate change are just some of the factors that will continue to relentlessly influence and challenge the MICE industry. In this complex field of tension, it's especially the MICE suppliers who find themselves in a quandary. Their distribution structures and business models, often still rooted in the past, are proving increasingly inadequate to meet modern requirements and rapidly changing demands. The growing shift from business travel to video calls, from corporate events to online events, and the reduction in participant numbers at hybrid events, pose new challenges that require a fundamental realignment of the industry.

The central challenge lies in balancing sustainability with economic viability. MICE suppliers are tasked with adapting their business models to not only meet economic demands but also address the ecological and social aspects of modern business life. This requires a rethink across the entire industry, strategic planning, and the willingness to leave traditional paths and embrace innovative approaches. Only through such transformation can MICE providers secure their relevance in the future and contribute valuably to the development of a sustainable and responsible event culture.

HYBRID EVENTS: A STRATEGIC TURN IN MICE SALES

With the onset of the pandemic, the MICE industry experienced an unprecedented shift in its sales strategies. The industry, traditionally focused on personal contact, had to abruptly adapt to a virtual environment due to global restrictions. This chapter explores the challenges and learning processes that MICE sales underwent during this transitional period and considers the role of hybrid events as a strategic measure for the future development of sales in this sector.

At the outset of the pandemic-induced restrictions, MICE sales seemed to find a quick solution in transferring events to online platforms like MS Teams, Zoom, and other video-call services. The initial response to these virtual events was positive, seemingly validating the concept. Event planners were receiving invitations to various online events almost daily, indicating the industry's effort to maintain contact and business relationships. However, enthusiasm for these virtual meetings quickly waned. The constant influx of invitations and the monotony of online interactions led to a rapid decline in interest from targeted event planners. Despite providers' increased efforts to encourage participation with additional incentives like gin, wine, whiskey, cakes, gifts, and even cash, the valuable and authentic interaction crucial to MICE sales was missing. The virtual approach failed to deliver the promise of genuine face-to-face interactions, leaving the industry in a dilemma.

The shift from real to virtual events exposed a credibility gap. The old MICE sales credo "Nothing beats the Face-to-Face Appointment" sharply contrasted with the new reality of virtual meetings. The challenge was not only to create the technical prerequisites for virtual events but also to fulfill the fundamental need for genuine, personal connection – a key feature that distinguishes the MICE industry.

In the search for a more balanced approach, hybrid events are becoming the focus as a strategic measure for MICE sales. Hybrid events combine the benefits of real and virtual formats, offering a flexible, integrative solution. They allow preserving the intimacy and immediacy of personal meetings while leveraging the reach and accessibility of virtual platforms. However, organizing hybrid events requires deeper strategic planning and a rethinking of sales approaches. It's essential to meaningfully combine the advantages of both formats and design interaction that sparks genuine interest and strengthens the value of the relationship between providers and event planners. This involves careful content selection, optimizing participant experience, and integrating interactive elements that resonate with both real and virtual attendees.

The pandemic era has posed unprecedented challenges for MICE sales and provided valuable insights into the importance of real connections and the need for a flexible, integrative approach. Hybrid events represent a promising strategic measure with the potential to lead MICE sales into a new era. By combining the strengths of real and virtual formats and focusing on genuine, valuable interactions, hybrid events can revolutionize how the MICE industry conducts business and builds relationships. The future requires a wise balance between technology and human touch – a balance achievable through carefully planned hybrid events.

CHALLENGES OF MICE SALES IN THE ONLINE AND HYBRID EVENT LANDSCAPE

The MICE industry has traditionally emphasized personal contact, deemed essential for building business relationships and generating leads. However, the transition to online events and the introduction of hybrid formats have created new challenges and opportunities that have proven complex to navigate and exploit. Adapting to these digital formats presents various challenges for MICE sales.

MISUNDERSTANDINGS AND OBSTACLES IN DIGITAL MICE SALES

The initial difficulties MICE sales faced with online events can be attributed to a fundamental misconception: the assumption that established personal sales strategies and techniques could be directly transferred to online formats. Reality showed that the digital world has its own rules and dynamics. The necessary registration and sign-up for online events, coupled with the need to block calendar slots and log in punctually, often became barriers and led to a rapid decline in interest from potential participants. This chain of obstacles highlights how quickly interest in an event can wane if the registration process is too complex or time-consuming. Another significant hurdle is the lack of utilization of social media platforms like YouTube Live, LinkedIn, Facebook Live, Twitch, Instagram, Threads, Bluesky or Twitter (X). These platforms offer immense reach and the ability to share content with a vast audience, both live and through recordings. The search engine presence of this content can also significantly increase the visibility and reach of an event. Despite this incredible potential, it was often not utilized, mainly because the organizers did not have direct access to the viewers' email addresses. This fixation on email collection as the primary goal of the lead generation process led to broader and potentially more valuable opportunities of social media being overlooked. The challenges and partial failures of MICE sales in the online world quickly led to a return to the old sales credo: "Nothing beats the Face-to-Face Appointment." This mentality underscores the long-standing preference for personal meetings and relationships in the MICE industry and highlights the difficulties associated with transitioning to digital sales strategies.

THE WAY FORWARD: HYBRID EVENTS IN MICE SALES

Despite initial difficulties, hybrid events offer a promising opportunity for MICE sales to expand their reach and develop new sales strategies. Some forward-thinking companies have begun broadcasting their webinars and online events on social media channels, leading to notable successes. The hybridization of sales measures offers numerous benefits: content originally intended for a closed audience can be made accessible to a broader audience. This not only increases the providers' visibility but also generates social selling and concrete business inquiries. Moreover, such approaches align with contemporary and classically hybrid sales measures by strategically combining the benefits of both worlds – online and offline. Integrating digital and hybrid formats into MICE sales is not a simple process and requires a thorough overhaul of existing strategies and mindsets. The industry faces the challenge of moving away from traditional sales methods and fully exploiting the potential of digital and hybrid events. Through strategic realignment, social media utilization, and a focus on genuine added value instead of mere lead generation, MICE sales can thrive in the digital era and create new success stories.

EMBRACING HYBRID EVENTS – THE PINNACLE OF STRATEGIC EVOLUTION IN MICE SALES

As we stand at the cusp of transformation in the MICE industry, the emergence of hybrid events has catalysed a strategic pivot, redefining the landscape of event planning and sales. This chapter encapsulates the essence of our journey through the dynamic world of MICE sales, emphasizing the profound potential of hybrid events when meticulously crafted and strategically implemented. It underscores the future of MICE sales as it transitions towards a sophisticated 'Hybrid Sales' model, underpinned by the pillars of content marketing, storytelling, and social media, blending the realms of social selling and personal selling into a cohesive and potent strategy.

Hybrid events, an ingenious amalgamation of in-person and virtual experiences, have surged to prominence, not as mere stopgap solutions but as pioneering models that offer fantastic options for event planners. They mark a significant leap from traditional formats, propelled by the digital revolution and the compelling need for versatility in the face of global challenges such as the Covid-19 pandemic. These multifaceted events harness the best of both worlds, combining the irreplaceable value of face-to-face interaction with the expansive reach and convenience of digital platforms.

The power of hybrid events lies in their ability to create immersive experiences that resonate with attendees, irrespective of their physical location. They provide a flexible framework that accommodates varying participant preferences, ensuring inclusivity and enhancing engagement. However, the true efficacy of hybrid events is contingent upon their meticulous planning and execution, integrating innovative technology, engaging content, and seamless logistics to deliver a cohesive and impactful experience.

Transitioning to a 'Hybrid Sales' model signifies a monumental shift in the MICE industry. It demands a strategic reorientation, moving beyond conventional sales tactics to embrace a holistic approach that leverages the synergies of content marketing, storytelling, and social media. This model advocates for crafting compelling narratives that captivate the audience, creating meaningful content that educates, informs, and entertains, and harnessing the power of social platforms to amplify reach and foster community engagement.

Content marketing emerges as a cornerstone in this new paradigm, offering a platform to articulate the unique value proposition of events, share insights and knowledge, and establish thought leadership. It paves the way for building trust and credibility with the audience, setting the stage for more profound and enduring relationships.

Storytelling, an age-old art, finds renewed significance in the context of hybrid events. It enables planners to weave a narrative that binds the audience, evoking emotions, and driving engagement. Through compelling storytelling, events transform into memorable experiences that leave a lasting imprint on the participants' minds.

Social media stands as a powerful ally in the Hybrid Sales model, providing unparalleled opportunities for outreach, interaction, and feedback. It facilitates real-time engagement, fosters community building, and offers invaluable insights into audience preferences and behaviors. By strategically leveraging social media, MICE sales professionals can enhance visibility, generate leads, and nurture relationships, all contributing to a robust sales funnel.

As we look ahead, the future of MICE sales appears promising and vibrant, illuminated by the prospects of Hybrid Sales. This innovative model, with its foundation in content marketing, storytelling, and social media, offers a roadmap for navigating the evolving landscape of event planning and sales. It calls for a paradigm shift, urging professionals to embrace change, harness technology, and focus on creating value-driven, engaging, and inclusive event experiences.

Hybrid events and the Hybrid Sales model herald a new era in the MICE industry, one that is adaptive, resilient, and forward-looking. As we embrace this transformative journey, we unlock the potential to craft events that are not just meetings or conferences but compelling narratives that inspire, connect, and endure. The future beckons with a promise of endless possibilities, and it is our strategic acumen, creativity, and commitment to excellence that will steer us towards new horizons in the MICE industry.

ABOUT THE AUTHOR

Peter Cramer's extensive career in the event management and communication industry is a testament to his expertise and innovation. Starting in 1992 as the Owner of Cramer & Möller, he spent over eight years in Hagen, managing and growing the company. In 2001, he transitioned to Ercom AG as an Event Manager, where he was responsible for the design, organization, and execution of various events, road shows, and exhibitions, honing his skills in Mainz for over three years.

His journey continued in 2004 at Publicis, a well-known worldwide communications agency in Hamburg. As a Senior Event Manager, Cramer was instrumental in designing, organizing, and implementing events, promotions, and sales promotion measures, demonstrating his ability to handle multiple aspects of event management.
In October 2006, he stepped up as the Director of Event Marketing at Publicis, where he spent nearly two years in Erlangen and München. His role involved the creation and design of integrated communication actions with a focus on event-centric strategies.

Cramer's expertise led him to achtung! erlebnis in November 2008, where he was the Unit Lead Manager for over a year.

Here, he was responsible for the development and management of the event unit, emphasizing integrative and holistic communication strategies.

Since March 2010, Peter Cramer has been the owner of Panem et Circenses - Kontor für Kommunikation in Hamburg. His company offers a comprehensive range of services in digital content marketing, social media marketing, and event marketing, focusing on B2C / B2B tourism and MICE/business tourism. His work targets the German-speaking markets of Germany, Austria, and Switzerland, providing market research, communication campaign conception, and the planning and implementation of various events.

Parallel to this, since March 2012, Cramer has also been involved in Product Management at MICEboard. This platform is a significant community for event planners in the German-speaking regions, offering information on international events and suppliers. MICEboard is known for its innovative approach, providing directories of qualified suppliers and informing planners through podcasts and stream tv.

Throughout his career, Peter Cramer has demonstrated a consistent ability to lead and innovate in the dynamic field of event management and communication, making significant contributions to the industry. His experience ranges from hands-on event planning to strategic management and development of comprehensive communication campaigns, making him a distinguished figure in his field.